TOP OF THE FOOD CHAIN

ALLIGATOR

KILLER KING OF THE SWAMP

ANGELA ROYSTON

WINDMILL BOOKS
New York

Published in 2014 by Windmill Books, An Imprint of Rosen Publishing
29 East 21st Street, New York, NY 10010

Produced for Windmill by Calcium Creative Ltd
Editor for Calcium Creative Ltd: Sarah Eason
US Editor: Sara Howell
Designers: Paul Myerscough and Keith Williams

Photo credits: Dreamstime: Asterixvs 9t, Blfink 14, Johan63 7b, John Anderson
Photo 9b, Kenneystudios 11t, Krisgun01 15b, Megasquib 20, Mikephotos 21b,
Mokreations 17b, Mtilghma 21t, Nelson Creative 16, Photophreak 11t, 15t,
Sohadiszno 6, Warren Price Photography 29r; Shutterstock: Nick Barounis
11b, Chunni4691 7t, Cameron Cross 5t, FloridaStock 1, 23, Goodluz 10, Shane
Gross 28, Arto Hakola 18, Cyrus Harn 19, Iofoto 27t, Eduard Ionescu 24, Heiko
Kiera cover, Brian Lasenby 13b, 29l, Delmas Lehman 4, Michelle D. Milliman 8,
Dennis Molenaar 5b, Neftali 26, R.A.R. de Bruijn Holding BV 27m, Saddako 12,
22, Stephen 17t, Vedderman123 25.

Library of Congress Cataloging-in-Publication Data

Royston, Angela, 1945–
 Alligator : killer king of the swamp / by Angela Royston.
      pages cm. — (Top of the food chain)
Includes index.
ISBN 978-1-61533-742-2   — ISBN 978-1-61533-801-6 (pbk.) —
ISBN 978-1-61533-802-3
1. Alligators—Juvenile literature. 2. Predatory animals—Juvenile literature. I.
Title.
QL666.C925R69 2014
597.98'4—dc23
                                2013002092

Manufactured in the United States of America

CPSIA Compliance Information: Batch #BS13WM: For Further Information contact Windmill Books, New York, New York at 1-866-478-0556

CONTENTS

Alligators are at home in the swamps and **wetlands** of the southeastern United States. They are most common in Louisiana and Florida, where you may often see one sunning itself on the edge of a river or lake. Be careful if you do spot one. Others may be hiding under the water!

Alligators are meat eaters. They hunt other animals that live in the wetlands. Their **prey** includes fish and animals that come to the waterside to drink. Together, alligators and their prey form a chain, with the alligator at the top. However, none of the animals in the food chain would be able to survive without the plants at the bottom of the chain.

Alligators lurk in the water in slow-flowing rivers and in lakes.

4

Plants and trees grow thickly in the swamps. Alligators and their prey hide near them.

Links in the Food Chain

Alligators feed on birds, snails, and frogs as well as fish and bigger animals. An alligator swallows a fish, but the fish has already fed on smaller fish or shrimps. The smallest water animals feed on tiny plants called **plankton**, which are too small to see without a microscope.

Nutrias are a favorite food for alligators in Louisiana.

Alligators are **reptiles**. These are animals which breathe air and have a scaly skin. Reptiles warm themselves by taking in heat from their environment. Alligators belong to an animal family called crocodilians. Crocodilians live in hot, wet places and include crocodiles, alligators, **caimans**, and gharials.

There are two types of alligators, American alligators and Chinese alligators. Only a few Chinese alligators still survive in the wild. American alligators share their wetland home with caimans and American crocodiles. You can tell a crocodile from an alligator by its snout. A crocodile has a long narrow snout, while an alligator's snout is short and broad.

Most caimans live in tropical rivers and swamps in Central and South America.

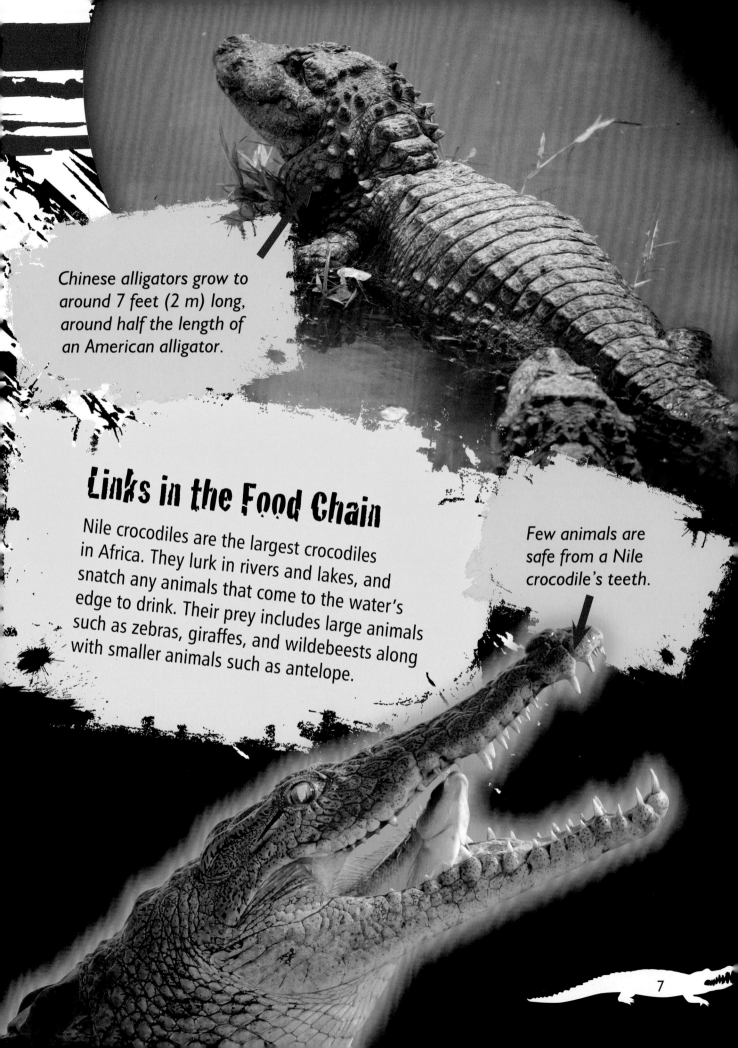

Chinese alligators grow to around 7 feet (2 m) long, around half the length of an American alligator.

Links in the Food Chain

Nile crocodiles are the largest crocodiles in Africa. They lurk in rivers and lakes, and snatch any animals that come to the water's edge to drink. Their prey includes large animals such as zebras, giraffes, and wildebeests along with smaller animals such as antelope.

Few animals are safe from a Nile crocodile's teeth.

TOP PREDATOR

An adult alligator is a top **predator** because it is perfectly designed to hunt and almost impossible to attack. It is a fast swimmer with incredibly strong jaws that it uses to grab its prey. Then its teeth get to work! An alligator's thick, scaly skin is like a suit of armor, which no other animal can pierce.

In addition to its weapons, an alligator has a good sense of smell and great eyesight and hearing. It uses all of these senses to find prey. Alligators also have an extraordinary extra sense. They can "feel" **vibrations** and slight movements in the water, which tell them when another animal is close by.

An alligator's scales are biggest along its back and tail and smallest on the sides of its head and its legs.

An alligator takes small animals and fish straight into its huge mouth and grabs big animals between its sharp teeth.

KILLER FACT

American alligators grow up to 15 feet (4.6 m) long and weigh up to 1,000 pounds (454 kg). An average-sized adult alligator is more than twice as long and more than four times as heavy than an average person!

Alligators have a big head, four short legs, and a long, strong tail.

LYING IN WAIT

One reason that alligators are such successful hunters is that they are not in a hurry. An alligator can lie in wait for hours with most of its body hidden beneath the water. It does not go looking for prey. It waits for its dinner to come to it!

Only the top of the alligator's head shows above the surface of the water, so its eyes can watch for prey and its nostrils can breathe in air. The alligator waits for prey to come near, either in water, on the land alongside the lake or river, or even in the air above its head. Then, when prey arrives, the predator goes into action!

An alligator hides among plants at the side of the river. It waits for prey to come within reach in the branches or in the water.

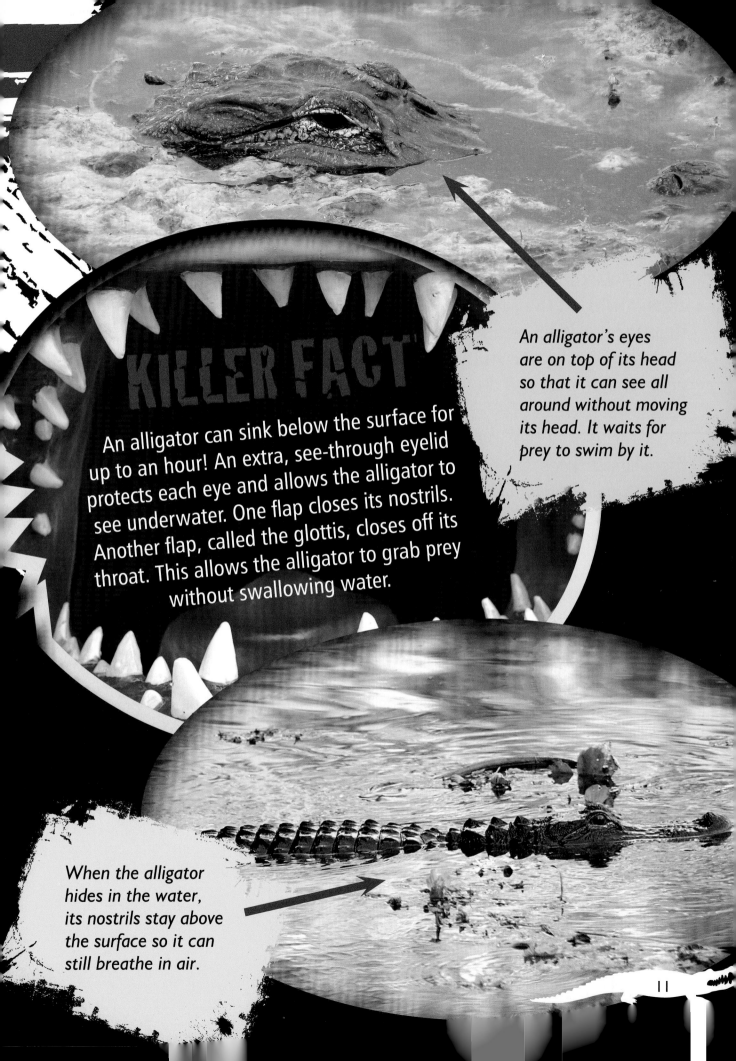

KILLER FACT

An alligator can sink below the surface for up to an hour! An extra, see-through eyelid protects each eye and allows the alligator to see underwater. One flap closes its nostrils. Another flap, called the glottis, closes off its throat. This allows the alligator to grab prey without swallowing water.

An alligator's eyes are on top of its head so that it can see all around without moving its head. It waits for prey to swim by it.

When the alligator hides in the water, its nostrils stay above the surface so it can still breathe in air.

THE KILL

An alligator attacks suddenly. If it senses prey in the water, it may just open its huge mouth and swallow it. It may also sink below the surface to grab larger prey from below. If an animal is on the riverbank, the alligator moves closer, then throws itself out of the water to snatch its prey.

When an alligator grabs a bigger animal, it drags the animal into the water. There it rolls over with its prey and holds it under the surface until the animal drowns. Then the alligator uses its powerful jaws to bite into the animal's body and rip off a chunk of flesh to swallow.

Even young alligators are not safe from adult alligators! This young alligator is about to be eaten by an older alligator.

Water snakes live alongside alligators in Louisiana and Florida. The snakes are eaten by alligators.

Links in the Food Chain

Alligators catch fish, turtles, water snakes, and small mammals in the water. Some water snakes, such as the Burmese python, are large enough to fight back. Burmese pythons are moving into the wetlands, but so far alligators have been able to stop them from taking over their territory.

An American anhinga is a water bird that feeds on fish. The bird is eaten by alligators.

FAST MOVER

Alligators use speed to catch their prey. They can move quickly in the water and on land. They swim by moving their strong tails from side to side. They also use their feet, which are partly **webbed**, to push them through the water.

Alligators run quickly on land by pushing against the ground with their legs and feet and twisting their bodies from side to side. They can run up to around 9 miles per hour (14 km/h), which is more than twice as fast as a person can move if walking quickly. You would have to run to get away from an alligator!

When an alligator strikes, it moves swiftly through the water toward its prey.

An alligator has long, sharp claws, which dig into the ground to pull it along on dry land.

An alligator can leap out of the water to catch prey above. This duck is being dangled over the water to tempt the alligators below.

KILLER FACT

Even birds and animals hiding in trees that hang over the water are not safe from alligators! An alligator's tail is so strong it can jump out of the water to catch a bird flying close to the surface, or to snatch prey from low branches above the water.

An alligator's jaws and teeth are its most terrifying weapons. Its jaws are so powerful they can crush bones and the shells of turtles! Although the muscles that shut an alligator's jaws are extremely strong, the muscles that open them are very weak. This is why a person can hold an alligator's jaws shut with just one hand.

An alligator's long jaws contain up to 80 teeth, which it uses to grip and then crush its prey. When a tooth becomes worn down, it falls out and a new one grows in its place. By the end of its life, an alligator may have used up 3,000 razor-sharp teeth.

Alligators use their teeth to snatch prey, crush bones and shells, and tear off chunks of flesh.

This man is holding an alligator's jaws closed. The alligator's muscles are not strong enough to open its mouth and bite him.

Links in the Food Chain

Turtles are well protected from most water animals, but not alligators! An alligator swallows small turtles, but also catches and crunches up larger ones. Turtles feed mainly on fish, although some feed only on plants.

A box turtle keeps out of the way as a huge alligator walks by.

Along with having a tough, scaly skin, an alligator is also protected by bony plates that form a suit of armor under its skin. It is almost impossible for another animal to pierce an alligator's armor or the ridge of bones along its back.

An alligator's skin is useful in other ways, too. Although it is tough, the skin is **sensitive** to tiny movements in the water. With its bumpy skin and dull brown or gray color, an alligator is well **camouflaged** as it lies in wait for its prey. It looks just like a log floating below the surface of the water, until it bursts to life and attacks its unsuspecting prey!

An alligator is covered with tough scales that fit closely together.

In murky water an alligator looks just like a rotting log. Its bumpy skin looks like a tree's rough bark.

KILLER FACT

Adult alligators are rarely attacked, but young alligators often are. Their main predators are turtles and other alligators. A large, stout turtle called an alligator-snapping turtle doesn't just snap at alligators. It eats smaller ones, too.

BABY ALLIGATORS

Unlike most reptiles, alligators take care of their young. A female alligator lays 20 to 60 eggs in a nest of rotting plants. She then stays close to the nest, chasing off raccoons and other animals that come near to it.

When the baby alligators are ready to **hatch**, they start to chirp. This is a signal for the mother to uncover the nest. Once the babies have hatched, the mother alligator carries them in her mouth to the water. The babies are very small when they hatch, only around 9 inches (22 cm) long. Their mother looks after them until they are around a year old.

Baby alligators cling to their mother's back as she swims through the water.

Links in the Food Chain

Baby alligators can swim and hunt from the moment they hatch. They stay close to their mother while they hunt, snapping up small fish, water snails, and other little water animals. The babies must be careful, though. Many animals, including turtles, raccoons, snakes, and wading birds, prey on them.

Life is dangerous for baby alligators. They keep together in groups, but only about one in five survive to become an adult.

Alligators can live to be around 50 years old in the wild.

HEAT CONTROL

Like all reptiles, alligators are **cold-blooded**. This means that they cannot use their own energy to make heat, but instead take in heat from their surroundings. Alligators are most active and able to hunt when they are warm, so they often **bask** in the sunlight to warm up their bodies.

When its surroundings cool down, an alligator slows down. When it becomes very cold, the alligator becomes **dormant**, which means it stops moving around. To make a place in which to rest, the alligator digs out a hole in the bank of a lake or river. These holes are called "gator holes." Alligators also dig holes in the mud to keep cool when it is hot.

Before they can get going in the morning, alligators warm up their bodies by lying in the sunshine.

KILLER FACT

Alligators do not use energy to keep themselves warm, which means they do not have to eat as much as other animals. For example, an alligator that weighs 800 pounds (362 kg) eats less than a 100-pound-(45 kg) dog.

If an alligator becomes too hot, it opens its mouth wide! This cools it down, just as panting helps a dog to cool down.

GREAT SURVIVOR

With their armored bodies and huge jaws, alligators look like ancient beasts, and they are! The first alligator lived around 35 million years ago, but their ancient relatives have been around since the age of the dinosaurs, around 200 million years ago.

The first crocodilians were land animals that had huge jaws. Later, they **evolved** and changed into creatures that could swim. These animals then continued to live in and out of water. Amazingly, alligators even survived the disaster that wiped out the dinosaurs and other animals 65 million years ago! They probably survived because they could lie low in freshwater and they could become dormant in times of cold and **drought**.

Many crocodile and alligator teeth survive as fossils. This fossil tooth belonged to an ancient crocodile that lived millions of years ago.

KILLER FACT

Crocodilians have several strengths that may have helped them to survive when the dinosaurs did not. Crocodilians are very tough and can quickly change to suit their environment. They also eat whatever they find, and can even survive for up to a year without eating!

This ancient alligator fossil was found in rock. It includes many sharp teeth and the long bones that formed the animal's jaws.

In the 1960s, American alligators became **endangered** because people hunted and killed them for their skin. In the 1970s and 1980s, laws were passed to protect alligators. Since then, American alligators have recovered so well that there are now more than 1 million alligators in the United States.

Chinese alligators are an endangered species. Fewer than 150 of them still live in the wild, living in just a few ponds along the banks of the Yangtze River in China. Local people hunt them because they say the alligators eat too many fish. Most Chinese alligators now live in **captivity**, in zoos around the world and in special centers where they can breed.

This postage stamp was made in the 1970s to tell people that laws needed to be passed to protect alligators.

US 3¢ ALLIGATOR

WILDLIFE CONSERVATION

Protected Area All Plant, Animal and Cultural Resources Protected or Regulated.

Area Protegida Todas las Plantas, Animales y Recursos Naturales son Protegidos o estan bajo Regulaciones.

Alligator Safety
Seguridad Relacionada a los Caimanes

It is illegal to feed or harass wildlife. *Do not approach Alligators.*

Es ilegal alimentar o molestar la vida silvestre.
No se acerque a los caimanes.

A sign in Everglades National Park tells visitors that alligators can be dangerous.

In the 1950s bags made of alligator skin were very fashionable.

KILLER FACT

In the past, alligator skins were sold for high prices. They were made into expensive goods, such as purses and shoes. In the United States today, it is illegal to kill an alligator, or to buy or sell its skin.

You might think that removing alligators would help other animals in the wetlands. In fact, the opposite is true because top predators help to keep the whole **habitat** healthy. People have discovered that protecting alligators keeps food chains in balance and helps to preserve the alligator's habitat.

When alligators almost became **extinct** in wetlands, the numbers of muskrats and nutrias in the area grew. These animals ate the river plants and damaged the wetland. After alligators were reintroduced to wetlands, they preyed on the muskrats and nutrias and kept their numbers in check. Gator holes made by alligators also help the wetlands. They are places where plants can grow and animals can shelter during drought.

When there are few or no alligators, the number of muskrats increases. They damage the wetland habitat by eating too many plants.

KILLER FACT

People threaten alligators, but alligators rarely attack human beings. In Florida, the US state that has the most alligators, only five people were killed between 1973 and 1990. In South Carolina only 11 people have reported being bitten by an alligator since 1948, and no one has been killed.

Alligator Safety

It is illegal to feed or harass wildlife.

Do not approach Alligators

For Your Safety: Please stay at least 25 feet from the wildlife!

Alligators make spaces called gator holes among plants. Gator holes hold water even during a drought, which helps other animals to survive.

Signs in wildlife refuges warn people not to feed or annoy the alligators.

GLOSSARY

bask (BASK) To sunbathe.

caimans (KAY-menz) A type of crocodilian that is smaller than an alligator.

camouflaged (KA-muh-flahzd) Hard to see because the coloring blends into the surroundings.

captivity (kap-TIH-vih-tee) When an animal is kept in a particular space and not in the wild.

cold-blooded (KOHLD-bluh-did) When an animal is unable to use its own energy to warm its blood and so is unable to keep itself warm. Reptiles, fish, and insects are all cold-blooded, but birds and mammals are warm-blooded.

dormant (DOR-ment) To be inactive but still alive.

drought (DROWT) A long period of time without much rain.

endangered (in-DAYN-jerd) When the number of surviving animals is so low that the animals are in danger of becoming extinct.

evolved (ih-VOLVD) Changed over a long period of time.

extinct (ik-STINGKT) No longer existing.

habitat (HA-buh-tat) The natural environment in which a living thing is found.

hatch (HACH) To break out of an egg.

nutrias (NOO-tree-uhz) Rodents (animals with large teeth that like to gnaw) that live in water.

plankton (PLANK-ten) Tiny plants and animals that float near the surface of water, but which are so small they can only be seen through a microscope.

predator (PREH-duh-ter) An animal that hunts other animals for food.

prey (PRAY) An animal or animals that are hunted by other animals.

reptiles (REP-tylz) A group of cold-blooded animals that have scaly skins and breathe in air.

sensitive (SEN-sih-tiv) Aware of.

vibrations (vy-BRAY-shunz) Tiny repeated movements.

webbed (WEBD) Having a thin layer of skin between the toes.

wetlands (WET-landz) Areas of wet ground, such as a swamp or marsh, or stretches of water such as ponds, rivers, lakes, and canals.

FURTHER READING

Baxter, Bethany. *Caimans, Gharials, Alligators, and Crocodiles.* Awesome Armored Animals. New York: PowerKids Press, 2014.

Bredeson, Carmen. *Fun Facts About Alligators!.* I Like Reptiles and Amphibians!. Berkeley Heights, NJ: Enslow Publishers, 2009.

Kalman, Bobbie. *Wetland Food Chains.* New York: Crabtree Publishing, 2006.

Rockwood, Leigh. *Tell Me the Difference Between an Alligator and a Crocodile.* How Are They Different?. New York: PowerKids Press, 2013.

WEBSITES

For web resources related to the subject of this book, go to: www.windmillbooks.com/weblinks and select this book's title.

INDEX